WORLD CULTURES

Living in the
Himalaya

Louise and Richard Spilsbury

Chicago, Illinois

© 2008 Raintree
Published by Raintree,
a division of Reed Elsevier Inc.
Chicago, Illinois

Customer Service 888–454–2279

Visit our website at www.heinemannraintree.com

Designed by Richard Parker and Manhattan Design
Printed and bound in China by SCPC

12 11 10 09 08
10 9 8 7 6 5 4 3 2 1

Library of Congress Cataloging-in-Publication Data
Spilsbury, Louise and Richard.
Living in the Himalaya.
p. cm. -- (World cultures)
Includes bibliographical references and index.
ISBN-13: 978-1-4109-2818-4 (library binding–hardcover)
ISBN-10: 1-4109-2818-7 (library binding–hardcover)
ISBN-13: 978-1-4109-2827-6 (pbk.)
ISBN-10: 1-4109-2827-6 (pbk.)
1. Sherpa (Nepalese people)--Social life and customs-
Juvenile literature. 2. Himalaya Mountains Region--
Social life and customs--Juvenile literature. I. Spilsbury,
Richard, 1963- II. Title.
DS493.9.S5S75 2007
305.895'41--dc22

2006037155

Acknowledgments
The publishers would like to thank the following for
permission to reproduce photographs: Alamy Images
pp. **15** (Urban Golob), **13** (Chloe Hall); Aurora Photos/
Robb Kendrick p. **19**; Corbis pp. **11** (Michael S. Lewis), **12**
(Alison Wright); Ecoscene/ Chinch Gryniewicz pp. **5, 28**;
Eye Ubiquitous/ Hutchison Picture Library p. **18**; Frances
Klatzel pp. **4, 7, 8, 9, 14, 17, 20, 27**; iStockPhoto/ Jose
Fuente pp. **22, 29**; Lonely Planet Images/ Richard I'Anson
pp. **24, 25**; Photolibrary/ Paul Franklin p. **10**; Robert
Harding Picture Library/ Alison Wright p. **16**; Travel Ink/
William Gray p. **26**.

Illustrations by International Mapping.

Cover photograph of a Sherpa woman carrying a basket
along a mountain path, reproduced with permission of
Photolibrary/Photononstop.

The publishers would like to thank Frances Klatzel for
her assistance with the preparation of this book.

Every effort has been made to contact copyright holders
of any material reproduced in this book. Any omissions
will be rectified in subsequent printings if notice is given
to the publishers.

Contents

Some words are printed in bold, **like this**. You can find out what they mean on page 31.

Mountain People

The Himalaya are a range (group) of mountains in Asia (see map on page 6). Some of the mountains are in the small country of **Nepal**. This is where Sherpa people live.

In the past

The first Sherpas arrived in Nepal over 500 years ago. They came from the country of Tibet. They built homes in the **valleys**. Valleys are the low areas between mountains.

Sherpas kept herds of large oxen called **yaks**. Yaks are grass-eating animals. They provided Sherpas with milk and wool. Sherpas also grew **crops** for food.

▶ A group of Sherpa people gathers for the *Mani Rimdu* festival (see page 25) to watch some dancers.

It is cold in the Himalaya. This yak's warm, long hair helps it survive.

Sherpas today

Some Sherpas are still farmers. Yaks and *dzopchioks* carry their loads. *Dzopchioks* are a cross between a yak and a cow. Many Sherpas work in tourism. They guide **trekkers** (climbers) across the mountains. Others have moved to work in cities such as Kathmandu.

SHERPA BELIEFS

Sherpas are **Buddhists**. Buddhists follow the teachings of a man called Buddha. They aim to live a good and happy life. Sherpas also believe that mountain gods protect them.

5

The Solu-Khumbu Region

Many Sherpas live in the Solu-Khumbu region. This area is in eastern **Nepal**. It has some of the highest **settlements** in the world! Settlements are places where people live.

High and cold

The Khumbu **valley**, in Solu-Khumbu, is very cold. At its highest points, there are few animals or plants. Lower down the valley, it is warmer. Here, you find forests where goats and deer live.

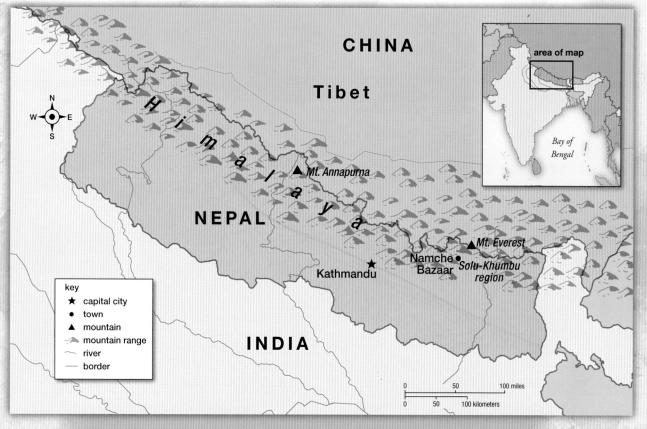

▲ The Solu-Khumbu region is just south of Mount Everest. Mount Everest is the highest mountain on Earth.

Mountain seasons

In this region, winter is from November to February. During winter, the village of Khumbu is under snow. Most Sherpas move their herds down the mountain.

In spring, the snow starts to melt. Sherpas move their herds back up to high **pastures**. Animals graze (feed) in these grassy areas.

▶ The houses in the village of Khumbu are built on the sloping mountainside.

CHANGING LANDSCAPES

Khumbu used to be colder than it is today. Sherpas built their first villages low down the valleys, where it was less cold. Today, the **climate** (weather) is warmer. This means Sherpas can now build higher up the mountain.

At Home

Many people in Khumbu live in stone houses. These usually have a sloped roof. This lets the rain and snow run off. The roofs are made of wooden planks or metal sheets. There are stones on top. The stones stop the roof from blowing off in strong winds.

Inside

Sherpas used to sleep in the same room. Families cooked on stoves or stone fireplaces. They lit candles for light.

Today, some homes have electricity. They use electric stoves, lights, refrigerators, TVs, and sometimes a computer. Some homes have separate bedrooms.

▶ These are Sherpa homes in the village of Khunde.

HOME ALTAR

Most Sherpa homes have a *lha-khang*. This is an **altar** (holy table). People light **incense** (perfume) and candles. They pray to pictures or statues of important religious teachers.

◄ Sherpa villages have no roads. Simple paths run between buildings and villages.

The village

There are different buildings in the village. Some villages have a health clinic, a school, or a market.

Villages in trekking areas have teahouses. Visitors use them to eat, sleep, and buy supplies, such as bottled drinks.

Sherpas grow some food in the Himalaya. Everything else they buy or **trade** (swap).

Crops and animals

Sherpas grow food such as potatoes, barley, and turnips. These **crops** survive the cold weather and poor mountain soil. Many Sherpas keep *dzooms*. *Dzooms* are female ***dzopchioks***. These animals are a cross between a **yak** and a cow. A yak's long hair helps it survive the cold. A cow makes lots of milk.

◄ Sherpas build terraced fields on the mountain slopes. The flat fields look like giant steps.

Favorite foods

Sherpas make butter, yogurt, and cheese from their animals' milk. They trade these at the market. They may buy rice, lentils, salt, eggs, spices, and meat. They also buy packaged foods such as instant noodles.

◀ This Sherpa woman is cooking a lunch of potatoes fried in delicious spices.

MEALS

A **traditional** Sherpa breakfast food is porridge. It is made from roasted barley flour, tea, and butter. Dinners are more filling. Dishes include buckwheat (cereal) mash and *shakpa*. *Shakpa* is a meat and vegetable stew with dumplings.

In a typical Sherpa family, the children, their mother, and their grandparents live together. The father is usually away for part of the year. He may be working on **treks** (journeys) with tourists or moving herds to different **pastures**.

▸ These Sherpa women are washing rice.

Chores

The whole family looks after the **crops** and animals. Everyone has chores to do. They wash clothes in the river and collect firewood from the forests. Sherpa girls usually do more household chores than boys. The grandparents may look after the youngest children while the mother cooks and shops.

12

Visitors

Sherpas often have visitors. In the mountains, it is a long distance from one village to another. People need places to stay in bad weather or after long journeys on foot. When Sherpa families have visitors, they may stay a long time.

▲ These Sherpa women share a drink made from millet, a crop they have grown.

GENEROSITY

When Sherpas offer visitors food or drink, they often say, "*Shey!*" or "*Shey-shey!*" This means, "Eat! Drink!"

The Community

Sherpas are one of several groups of people in **Nepal**. Everyone speaks some Nepali. This is the national language of Nepal. Each group also speaks a different language and has its own traditions.

◀ Here, a lama introduces families at a wedding ceremony.

SPIRIT BELIEFS

Some Sherpas visit a **lama** when their family is having difficulties. Lamas are **Buddhist** priests. They ask the spirits of places and dead people for help. They also advise people.

Helping hands

Two important people in a Sherpa community are the lama (see page 14) and the **herbalist**.

The herbalist treats illnesses with medicines. The medicines are made from mountain plants. Many Sherpas believe these remedies (treatments) work better than medicines from a health clinic.

▶ The biggest markets for Sherpas are in large towns. This market is at Namche Bazaar (see map on page 6).

Market meetings

The weekly markets are important for Sherpa people. These are often the only times Sherpas get together. This is because their **settlements** can be far apart.

Clothing

Mothers and grandparents usually wear **traditional** clothes. Traditional clothes are clothes that have looked the same for many years.

Keeping warm

Traditional Sherpa clothes were made to keep people warm in the cold Himalayan **environment** (surroundings). The *chuba* is a warm, ankle-length robe. It is made from **yak** wool. Other warm, woolen clothes include striped aprons, boots, and felt hats.

▲ Thick aprons protect these women's clothes while they work outdoors.

Changing clothes

Younger Sherpas usually wear modern clothes. Some families buy new jeans, skirts, and flip-flops from Tibetan traders (sellers). The traders bring the clothes from China. They sell them at markets.

Mountain guides are often given walking shoes and fleece clothes by **trekkers**.

JEWELRY

Some Sherpas wear traditional gold or silver necklaces and earrings. They include lumps of stone, such as turquoise from Tibet. Another example is red coral from the Mediterranean. The stones were **traded** by the Sherpas' **ancestors** (older relatives).

▶ A Sherpa woman wears large and colorful jewelry.

Learning

In the past, most Sherpa children were taught by their families, visitors, and **lamas**.

▲ Sherpa children work hard in a school classroom.

Today

Today, many Sherpa children go to school. Some walk along mountain paths to get there. It can take hours. A few children never go to school. They help on the family farm. Other parents cannot afford to pay school fees.

▲ Sherpas learn other languages from watching television and listening to the radio.

In school

Sherpa schools can be simple huts. They may have benches, a blackboard, and a few books. Bigger schools have libraries. Children learn reading, writing, and math.

At home

In the past, Sherpas mainly read **Buddhist** religious books. Today, they may also read newspapers and magazines. They learn English and other languages from **trekkers**. Some also have computers and surf the Internet.

LANGUAGES

Most school classes are taught in Nepali. This is the national language of **Nepal**. Some children also speak the Sherpa language. This is based on the language of Tibet.

Games and Storytelling

Sherpa children play tag, soccer, and volleyball. They fly kites and climb trees. They may also play *karem*. This is a square, wooden board game.

Young men and boys at the **monasteries** also play games. They ski on the snowy slopes. They construct skis from cardboard or old plastic water pipes!

▲ These young boys training to become **monks** are having fun.

Storytelling

Lamas and older people in the Sherpa community often tell stories. They tell many **traditional** stories and legends.

Many stories are about yetis. These **mythical** (imaginary) creatures are like large, hairy ape people. One story is about a kind yeti. A lama was praying in a mountain cave for several months. The kind yeti brought food and water to the lama. When the yeti died, its hand and scalp were kept in a special temple called a **gompa**.

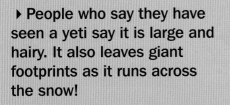

▶ People who say they have seen a yeti say it is large and hairy. It also leaves giant footprints as it runs across the snow!

21

Khumbu Legends

There are many legends about the Himalaya mountains where the Sherpas live.

Finding Khumbu

One legend tells the story of how the Sherpas chose to live in the Himalaya. In this legend, a man named Guru Ringpoche hid the Khumbu valley and other Himalayan **valleys**. Guru hid them for his people. He knew they were safe places where his people could live. Guru described Khumbu as a valley surrounded by snowy peaks in his religious books. This helped his people find the Himalayan valleys. According to legend, the first Sherpas found the Khumbu valley using Guru's directions.

▸ Mount Everest is one of the Himalaya mountains (see map on page 6).

MOUNTAIN GODDESS

For centuries the Sherpas and Tibetans have believed in five sister goddesses. These goddesses lived high up in the Himalaya mountains.

▶ Today, Sherpas believe the mountain goddess of Mount Everest brings happiness and good luck to people.

In the past, Sherpas believed it was wrong to climb Mount Everest. They thought it might upset the powerful goddess who lived there. When Sherpas first climbed the mountain, they made offerings (gave gifts) and prayed for her forgiveness.

A lot of **traditional** Sherpa music and dance happens at **gompas**. Gompas are temples found in a **monastery** or village.

Gompa orchestra

Lamas and **monks** play drums and cymbals. There are more unusual instruments, such as the long horn. Its deep, loud sound can be heard over great distances. It is made in sections that can slide inside each other, like a telescope. This helps mountain musicians carry it.

▸ The long horn is as long as a small car.

24

OM MANI PADME HUM

Sherpas chant the holy words *Om mani padme hum* when praying. Holy chants are called **mantras**. As **Buddhists**, Sherpas believe this mantra builds kindness and compassion.

▲ Dancers dress up as different characters in the *Mani Rimdu* festival.

Dance rituals

Mani Rimdu is a festival held twice a year. Many Sherpas **trek** (journey) for days to reach gompas and celebrate. Lamas dress in costumes and masks. They perform special dances that tell of Buddhism's triumph over evil. Noisy chanting and horns can be heard for miles around!

Special Occasions

The Sherpas in Khumbu enjoy celebrations and ceremonies at different times of the year.

Dumje

Dumje is a celebration. It is held at the start of the rainy **monsoon** season. Sherpas celebrate their unity and the birthday of an important Tibetan **Buddhist**. The village men gather together to pray and dance. They throw barley flour for good luck.

◀ The colors of Sherpa prayer flags have meaning. Blue is water, white is metal, red is fire, green is wood, and yellow is earth.

PRAYER FLAGS

Prayer flags are long strings with colorful cloth flags. They are printed with **mantras** (chants). Sherpas put up prayer flags. The flags help them with any new work they may be starting.

Naming ceremony

When a Sherpa baby is born, there is a naming ceremony. The parents hire a **lama** to choose the baby's name. The name is often the day it was born. For example, Pasang means Friday. Parents may also choose a name for their child.

▲ New parents attend a naming ceremony for their baby.

Can You Survive in the Himalaya?

Take this quiz to see how well you know the Himalaya after reading this book. If you score less than five, put your suitcase back in the closet! But if you score seven or more, you have a good chance of surviving a trip to the land of the Sherpa!

1. Where are the Himalaya?
A) Africa B) Europe C) Asia

*2. What are **yaks**?*
A) vegetables B) jewelry
C) animals that carry loads

*3. What is a **traditional** Sherpa breakfast?*
A) coffee B) toast C) porridge

4. What kind of roof should you build in the mountains?
A) flat   B) sloping C) either

5. Why do Sherpas farm in terraces?
A) to create flat fields B) they look nice C) yaks like them

6. Who should you go to if you get sick?
A) the **lama** B) the **herbalist** C) a yeti

7. Which is the highest mountain on Earth?
A) Mount Kenya B) Everest C) Snowdon

8. What do Sherpas do at their home **altars**?
A) pray and light **incense** B) eat dinner C) write letters

9. When Sherpas say, "Shey-shey," what do they mean?
A) Eat! Drink! B) Sit down C) Please leave!

10. What are printed on prayer flags?
A) **mantras** (chants) B) drawings C) poems

Find Out for Yourself

Books to read

Burleigh, Robert. *Tiger of the Snows: Tenzing Norgay: The Boy Whose Dream Was Everest*. New York: Atheneum, 2006.

Capua, Sarah de. *Mount Everest*. New York: Children's Press, 2002.

Morris, Neil. *Earth's Changing Mountains* (*Landscapes and People* series). Chicago: Raintree, 2004.

Websites

www.pbs.org/wgbh/nova/everest/history/sherpasworld.html
Find out more about the Sherpa people.

library.thinkquest.org/10131/nepal_sherpas.html
Look at where the Sherpa people live.

Glossary

altar table or surface on which offerings (gifts) to a god are made

ancestor parent, grandparent, great-grandparent, or any other past relative of a family

Buddhist person who follows the teachings of a man called Buddha

climate temperature or weather usually found in a place over a long time

crop food plant grown by farmers to eat or sell

dzopchiok animal that is a cross between a cow and a yak

environment surroundings

gompa temple found in each monastery or village

herbalist person who heals people using herb plants

incense perfumed substance that gives off its scent when burned

lama Buddhist priest

mantra holy chant

monastery place where monks live

monk boy or man who devotes his life to prayer and his religious beliefs

monsoon rainy season

mythical to do with legends or myths that have been told for years

Nepal country in South Asia, found high in the Himalaya

pasture area of grass where farm animals graze

settlement place where people have settled and built their homes

trade buying and selling to make a living

traditional something that has been done in the same way for many, many years

trek long, difficult journey

trekker person traveling a long way on foot for pleasure

valley long, low area of land, usually found between hills or mountains

yak large Tibetan ox

Index